# THE WORLD
## IN THE TIME OF
# CHARLEMAGNE

Belitha Press

## FIONA MACDONALD

First published in 1997 by

Belitha Press Limited, London House, Great
Eastern Wharf, Parkgate Road, London SW11 4NQ

Text by Fiona Macdonald
Map by Robin Carter, Wildlife Agency

ISBN 1 85561 703 X

British Library Cataloguing in Publication Data
for this book is available from the British Library.

Editor: Claire Edwards
Art Director: Helen James
Series Design: Roger Miller
Design: Rosamund Saunders
Picture Researcher: Diana Morris
Consultant: Sallie Purkis

Printed in Hong Kong
9 8 7 6 5 4 3 2 1

**Picture acknowledgements:**
AKG, London: 4 Eric Lessing; 6 St. Paul in
Lavanttal Klosterbibliothek; 11b & 35 Veintimilla.
Axiom: 14b C. Bradley.
Bridgeman Art Library: front cover c & 30 Bibliothèque Nationale
des Cartes et Plans, Paris; 1c & 16b Victoria & Albert Museum,
London; 3 & 5b Musée du Louvre, Paris; 13t Index; 17c Bonhams,
London; 19t British Library; 23b Bonhams, London;
31l Science Museum, London; 10bl &
45b Pitt Rivers Museum, Oxford.
C.M. Dixon: 7 British Museum; 10t, 10cbr,
12, 20t; 25c Ashmolean Museum, Oxford;
27t, 29t, 37t, 38b, 42, 43b.

**Picture acknowledgements cont.: E.T. Archive:** front cover r; 1l & 36
Archaeological Museum Cividale, Fruili; 2 & 18 Ashmolean Museum, Oxford;
5t Stiftbibliothek, St. Gall; 17t British Museum; 22b Freer Gallery of Art,
Washington D.C.; 24 British Museum; 27b Musée Cernuschi, Paris; 29b;
34 British Library; 37b Trinity College, Dublin; 43t Turkish Islamic
Museum, Istanbul.
**Werner Forman Archive:** back cover l & 40c Eskenazi Ltd., London;
cover drop-ins, 1r, 10c, 13c Universitetets Oldsaksamling, Oslo; 14t Biblioteca
Nacional, Madrid; 21t Museum of Mankind, London; 21b, 23t National
Museum of Anthropology, Mexico; 26; 11cb & 28t Idemitju Museum of
Art, Tokyo; 28b Arizona State Museum; 10c & 31r Private Collection;
11c & 32b National Comission for Museum & Monuments, Lagos; 38t
Mrs Bashir Mohamed Collection; 41t, 41b Private Collection, New York;
44, 10br & 45c Maxwell Museum of Anthropology, Albuquerque.
**Sonia Halliday Photographs:** 25b Bibliothèque Nationale, Paris.
**Michael Holford:** 16t.
**Hutchison Library:** 15; 22t Isabella Tree; 39.
**Scala, Florence:** 20b.
**Spectrum Colour Library:** 32t.
**Victoria & Albert Museum, London:** 33.

# CONTENTS

## ABOUT THIS BOOK

This book tells the story of Charlemagne, and also looks at what was happening all around the world in his time. To help you find your way through the book, each chapter has been divided into seven sections. Each section describes a different part of the world, and is headed by a colour bar. As you look through a chapter, the colour bars tell you which areas you can read about in the text below. There is a time line, to give you an outline of world events in Charlemagne's time, and also a map, which shows some of the most important places mentioned in this book.

On page 46 there is a list of some of the peoples you will come across in this book. Some of the more unfamiliar words are also listed in the glossary.

# THE STORY OF CHARLEMAGNE

Charlemagne reigned over a vast area of land in the region we now call Europe. As King of the Franks he ruled much of present-day France and Germany, and went on to conquer many other nearby peoples and lands. By the time he died he had founded a great empire that remained famous for more than a thousand years.

This book will tell you about life in Charlemagne's Europe and what was happening elsewhere in the world in Charlemagne's time. He was born in 742 and died, aged 71, in 814. This book looks at a slightly longer time span, from 700 to 900. It will help you to find out about some of the people, events and ideas that shaped the world before Charlemagne was born, and to discover what happened in the years after he died.

◀ This bronze statue, made in about 870, shows Charlemagne on horseback. He is wearing a crown, but is otherwise dressed in warrior's clothes. Charlemagne hated to wear rich silk robes. He preferred tough woollen tunics and leggings, and cloaks of rat and otter fur.

## KING OF THE FRANKS

Charlemagne was the son of Pepin the Short, King of the Franks, and Queen Bertrada. The Franks were a warlike people who lived in south-west Germany and France. When King Pepin died in 768 Charlemagne and his brother, Carloman, both became king. But Carloman died just three years later. From then on, Charlemagne ruled alone.

## BUILDING AN EMPIRE

The Frankish kingdom was rich and powerful. Charlemagne used its fierce, well-organized army to conquer land in present-day Italy, Austria and Hungary. For more than 30 years he also fought against the Saxons in northern Germany. Charlemagne used cruel tactics to conquer his enemies. Once he gave orders to execute 4,500 Saxons in a single day. He also tried to force them to follow the Christian faith. The punishment for those who refused was death. The Saxons were brave fighters, but eventually they surrendered. Charlemagne's only important failure was against Muslim Spain, which he never managed to conquer.

▲ Frankish soldiers riding into battle. They are wearing chain mail tunics, and carrying round wooden shields and long spears. The soldier at the front is holding a banner shaped like a dragon. This manuscript was painted in about 750.

## CROWNED ON CHRISTMAS DAY

By 800 Charlemagne had conquered so much land, he believed he was as powerful as the emperors of Ancient Rome. He travelled to Rome where the Pope, who was the head of the Christian Church in Western Europe, crowned him Holy Roman Emperor on Christmas Day.

## MARRYING FOR POWER

Charlemagne was married four times. He always chose women from powerful noble families, as a way of making important political alliances. After his last wife, Fastrada, died, Charlemagne spent the final years of his life with his girlfriend – a beautiful and very clever woman called Liutgard.

► Charlemagne wore this sword, called *Joyeuse* (Joyful), on special occasions, such as his coronation. It is decorated with gold and precious stones. Warriors at this time often gave their favourite weapons special names.

## CHARLEMAGNE THE LAW MAKER.

Charlemagne was not just a fearsome army commander. He was also a great law maker, and a patron of learning and the arts. He could speak Latin, as well as his own Frankish language, although he could not read or write. To help him learn, he kept writing-tablets (folding pieces of wood, covered with a thin layer of wax) under his pillow, so he could practise making the shapes of letters in the wax whenever he woke up at night.

## MONKS AND MANUSCRIPTS

Charlemagne never did learn to read, but he knew how useful reading and writing could be. He employed monks and priests to write down records of important events, make copies of peace treaties, send orders to royal officials and army commanders, and keep accounts of royal treasures and taxes. Charlemagne invited the best scholars in Europe to come and work for him in his palace at Aachen, a busy town on the borders of Germany and France. He appointed an English monk, named Alcuin, to supervise the training of his officials and scribes. Alcuin set up schools and libraries, and workshops for writing manuscripts.

◄ Charlemagne (on the left of the picture) is giving orders to his chamberlain, the official in charge of running the royal palace. The artist has shown how fine the palace was. It was designed with rounded arches and tall columns, decorated with carved stone designs.

► The pale pink area shows the Frankish empire. New land conquered by Charlemagne is shaded in dark pink. The lines show how modern France and Germany began to take shape when Charlemagne's empire was divided among his descendants in 870.

► A scribe at work, writing a manuscript. He is holding a pen made from reed in his right hand, and is dipping it into ink made of soot mixed with glue and oak gall (a growth found on some oak trees). Charlemagne's scholars trained the palace scribes to write in beautiful, clear handwriting.

## GOVERNING THE EMPIRE

Charlemagne let all the different people in his empire follow their own local customs and laws. But he appointed governors to rule over each separate district, to make sure that the conquered peoples stayed loyal. Twice a year the governors travelled to Charlemagne's palace to discuss problems and plan new laws. Lawyers at the palace also settled disputes between conquered peoples.

## WEIGHTS AND MEASURES

Charlemagne told his officials to encourage trade. He hoped this would link the different peoples he ruled more closely together. It also meant that he could collect taxes on goods being bought or sold. He repaired the old Roman roads that ran across Europe, and invented a system of weights, measures and coins to be used in all his lands.

## AFTER CHARLEMAGNE

After Charlemagne died, his empire was ruled by Louis, his only surviving son. Louis was also a successful warrior, but his three eldest sons quarrelled among themselves, and there were riots and rebellions. At the same time enemy armies from Viking countries and Spain invaded their lands. Gradually, under Louis and his sons, Charlemagne's empire began to fall apart.

## PRAISED AND FEARED

Charlemagne's name means Charles the Great, and he was larger than life in many ways. He was tall, strong and full of energy. He even lived longer than most people of his time. His friends praised his courage and his love of learning. His enemies feared his ruthless ambition and his cruelty in battle. But this mixture of qualities helped him to conquer and rule the biggest European empire since Roman times.

# THE WORLD 700-900

## ABOUT THE MAPS

The maps on this page will help you find your way around the world in Charlemagne's time. The big map shows some of the places mentioned in the text, including:

• **COUNTRIES** that are different from modern ones, such as Ife and Ghana (which is different from modern Ghana).

• *Past peoples*, such as the Franks and Celts.

• *Towns and cities.* To find the position of a town or city, look for the name in the list below then find the number on the map.

• *GEOGRAPHICAL FEATURES*, including mountains and rivers.

| | | |
|---|---|---|
| 1 Palenque | 8 Constantinople | 15 Ellora |
| 2 Bonampak | 9 Kiev | 16 Angkor |
| 3 Cahokia | 10 Fustat | 17 Borobodur |
| 4 Cordoba | 11 Damascus | 18 Chang'an |
| 5 Kumbi Saleh | 12 Baghdad | 19 Hangzhou |
| 6 Kairouan | 13 Mecca | 20 Kyoto |
| 7 Rome | 14 Samarkand | 21 Nara |

The little map shows the world divided into seven regions. The people who lived there were linked by customs, traditions, beliefs, or simply by their environment. There were many differences within each region, but the people living there had more in common with each other than with people elsewhere. Each region is shown in a different colour – the same colours are used in the headings throughout the book.

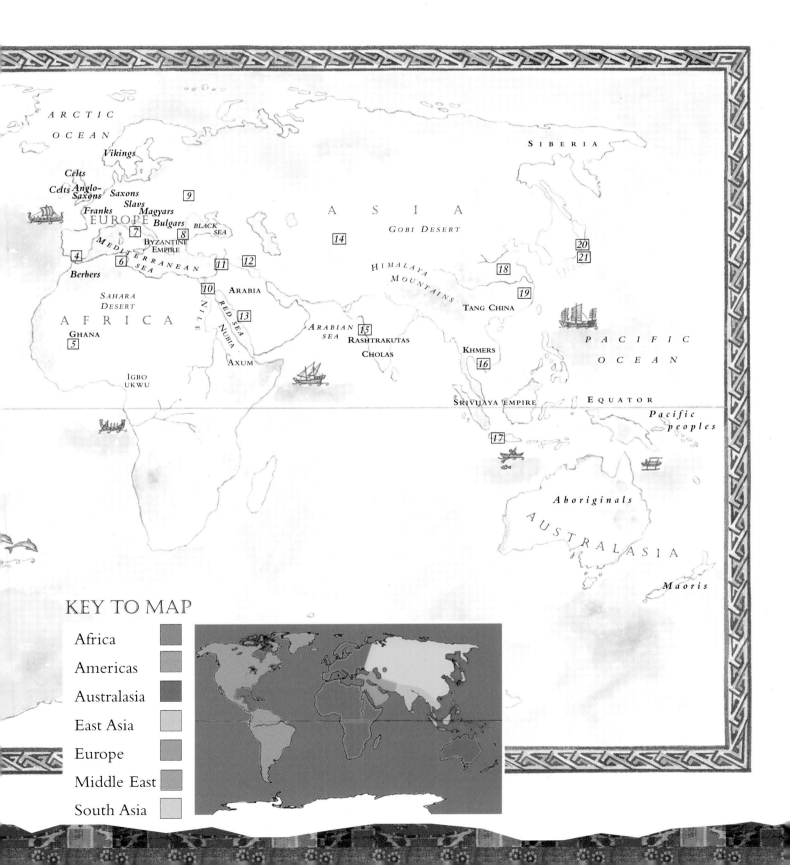

ARCTIC

OCEAN

SIBERIA

*Vikings*

*Celts*

*Celts* *Anglo-*
*Saxons* *Saxons*

*Slavs*

*Franks* *Magyars*

EUROPE *Bulgars*

7  8  BLACK
SEA

BYZANTINE
EMPIRE

4  6

MEDITERRANEAN
SEA

*Berbers*

11  12

10  ARABIA

NILE

RED SEA

SAHARA
DESERT

A F R I C A

NUBIA

13

GHANA

5

AXUM

*ARABIAN*
*SEA*

IGBO
UKWU

A  S  I  A

GOBI DESERT

14

HIMALAYA
MOUNTAINS

18

TANG CHINA

19

20
21

15

RASHTRAKUTAS

CHOLAS

KHMERS

16

PACIFIC

OCEAN

SRIVIJAYA EMPIRE

EQUATOR

*Pacific*
*peoples*

17

*Aboriginals*

AUSTRALASIA

*Maoris*

## KEY TO MAP

Africa

Americas

Australasia

East Asia

Europe

Middle East

South Asia

# TIME LINE

## EUROPE

**c.700** Anglo-Saxon poem called *Beowulf* composed. It is an adventure story about brave warriors fighting a monster.

**719–741** An English monk called St Boniface travels to Germany to spread the Christian faith.

**700s** Stirrups introduced to Europe from Central Asia.

**731** A monk called the Venerable Bede writes a *History of the English Church and People*. He is the first historian to date events from the birth of Jesus Christ.

**732** The Franks defeat Muslim armies at Tours, in France, and stop a Muslim invasion of Europe.

**742** Charlemagne born.

**757** Offa becomes King of Mercia (in English Midlands). From 779 he rules all southern England.

**771** Charlemagne becomes sole king of the Franks.

**773–4** Charlemagne conquers northern Italy.

## MIDDLE EAST

**712** Muslim armies conquer the rich trading city of Samarkand.

**712** Birth of Rabiyah al-Adawiyyah, Muslim woman scholar and mystic. She offers wise advice to people in Baghdad.

**718** Byzantine emperor Leo III defeats Muslim siege of Constantinople.

**762** Caliph al Mansur builds the city of Baghdad as a new capital for the Muslim empire.

**786–809** Caliph Harun al-Rashid rules over a rich court, where the royal family eat from dishes of silver and gold.

## AFRICA

**c.700** Muslim leaders rule most of North Africa.

**c.700** Trade in salt, gold and slaves across the Sahara Desert begins to increase.

**711** Muslim armies from North Africa set off to invade Spain.

**700s** Groups of Bantu peoples migrate to southern Africa, taking knowledge of advanced iron-working techniques with them.

**741–742** Berbers rebel against their Muslim rulers.

## SOUTH ASIA

**700s** Many Buddhists in southern India begin to follow the Hindu faith.

**712** Muslim armies set up a new state in Sind (present-day Pakistan).

**c.750** Hindu king, Dantidurga, defeats the Chalukyas and founds the Rashtrakuta dynasty.

**c.790** Ellora temple completed. It becomes an important religious centre, for Hindu and Buddhist pilgrims.

## EAST ASIA

**c.710** Site chosen at Nara for a new Japanese capital city.

**712–756** Rule of Emperor Tang Xuanzong, the Shining Emperor of the Tang dynasty.

**720** Chinese inventor I Hsing invents clockwork.

**730** Chinese inventors experiment with wood-block printing on paper.

**743** Buddhism becomes an official religion in Japan.

**748** First printed newspaper in China.

**751** Chinese defeat Muslim armies at Battle of Talas River. This stops further Muslim conquests in East Asia.

**770** Wood-block printing starts in Japan.

## AMERICAS

**c.700** First pueblos built by Anasazi people in south-west North America. Houses are made of sun-dried mud-brick.

**700s** People living in the Mississippi valley build mound-cities. They are North America's first towns.

**c.750** Mississippi people grow maize, weave cotton cloth, and build ball-courts and temple mounds in south-east North America.

**700s** Chimu begin to dominate the coast of present-day northern Peru.

## AUSTRALASIA

**c.700** Settlers by now well-established on Easter Island. They lived by hunting wild animals, by fishing along the coast, and by catching seabirds.

**c.700–900** Settlers on Hawaii divide the land into wide strips called ahupuaa, which stretch from the mountains down to the sea. This made sure that each family had a share of different types of land, to provide food all year round.

**800**                    **850**                    **900**

**793** First Viking attack on England.

**c.800** A manuscript of the four Gospels, called the *Book of Kells*, is made by monks and beautifully decorated in the Celtic style.

**800** Charlemagne crowned Holy Roman Emperor in Rome.

**814** Charlemagne dies.

**843** Kenneth MacAlpine unites Scottish and Pictish states to create kingdom of Scotland.

**845** Vikings raid Paris.

**c.850** Vikings begin to settle in northern and eastern England.

**c.870–874** First Viking settlements in Iceland.

**871** Alfred the Great becomes King of Wessex, England. He stops Viking conquest of south-west England.

**882** By this date the Vikings are ruling a settlement in Russia from their base at Kiev.

**c.900** The Muslims have introduced aubergines, apricots, sugar and almonds to southern Spain. Cordoba has become a great centre of arts and learning.

**797** Byzantine empress Irene blinds her son so that she can rule instead of him.

**811** Bulgar armies attack Byzantine Empire. They kill the emperor and make his skull into a drinking cup for their king.

**770–790** Under the rule of King Kaya Maghan Sisse, Ghana continues to grow powerful in West Africa.

**c.800** Kanem-Bornu empire begins to grow strong in West Africa.

**814** Muslim scholars begin to use Indian numbers (1 to 9) for mathematical calculations.

**862** A new way of writing, called the Cyrillic alphabet, introduced by Byzantine missionaries to Russia and nearby lands,

**836** The Great Mosque at Kairouan is built, then added to in 862 and 875.

**c.896** Magyar people from Central Asia reach borders of Middle East.

**c.900** A collection of Middle Eastern stories, *1001 Arabian Nights*, first written down. The setting is partly based on the court of Harun al-Rashid.

**868** Ibn Tulun sent to Egypt. He founds a new dynasty called the Tulunids.

**900** Height of Igbo Ukwu civilization in West Africa.

**c.800** Temple of Borobudur built in Java.

**802** Khmer king Jayavarman II begins to conquer a great empire in South-east Asia.

**800s** Srivijaya kings control ships travelling through the Strait of Malacca (in present-day Indonesia) and rule a rich trading empire.

**c.900** Khmer king Yashovarman I (889–c.910) builds his capital city at Angkor, in present-day Cambodia.

**779** Chinese scholar and food expert Lo Yu publishes *A Handbook of Tea*.

**794** New Japanese capital city built at Kyoto.

**800** By about this date, Chinese had perfected true porcelain, a type of hard, brilliant white china.

**842** Tibetan empire collapses.

**868** First-known printed book, the *Diamond Sutra*, made in China.

**875–884** Huang Ch'ao Rebellion against the emperor. This is a large scale rebellion in China, led by army generals who set up their own warlord states.

**c.800** Dorset civilization flourishes in Arctic regions of North America.

**c.800** Bright wall-paintings made to decorate Maya royal palace at Bonampak.

**c.800** Hunters in south-east North America begin to hunt with bows and arrows, instead of darts and spears.

**c.900** Yucatan (in present-day Mexico) becames new centre of Maya civilization.

**c.900** Toltec and Mixtec states begin to grow powerful in Central America.

**c.850–900** The first Maori settlers arrive in New Zealand, from other islands in the Pacific Ocean, and settle along the coast.

**700–900** Aboriginal people in Australia live by hunting, fishing, and gathering seeds, fruits and grubs. They build shelters and make canoes for fishing off the coast. In northern Australia, they trade with sailors from islands in the Indian Ocean.

Many of the dates shown in this Time Line are approximate. The letter c. stands for the Latin word *circa*, and means 'about'.

# AROUND THE WORLD

In Charlemagne's time there was almost constant warfare in many parts of the world. Villages and towns were attacked by enemy soldiers and in pirate raids. There were migrations of tribes who arrived in new lands and fought the people already living there. In Europe this period used to be called the Dark Ages, because of all the wars, and because so little written evidence survives. But historians now know this was also an exciting time. Brave explorers settled in the wild forests of Russia and on remote islands in the Pacific Ocean. Islam, a major new religion, spread from Arabia to southern Spain and to the borders of China. Artists created beautiful objects, and scholars spent their lives in study.

◄ This tombstone, from a church in Yorkshire, was made in about 900. It shows an English soldier – or perhaps a Viking warrior who had settled in England. He is wearing a pointed helmet and wide leather belt around his waist. You can see his long spear (left). On the right are his round shield (top), broad sword (middle) and battle-axe (bottom).

## LAND OF MANY KINGDOMS

EUROPE

When Charlemagne came to power, modern European countries like Britain, France and Germany did not exist. Instead Europe was divided into many different kingdoms. Often, the kingdoms were very small. There were seven Anglo-Saxon kingdoms in England, plus several Celtic kingdoms in Scotland, Ireland and Wales. These kingdoms fought one another. They also had to defend themselves against invaders. From about 800 onwards, Viking raiders from Scandinavia attacked communities in many parts of northern Europe. They established new Viking settlements in England, Scotland, Ireland, Finland, Russia and northern France.

▲ Part of a gold strip from a Celtic book-binding, looted by Viking raiders and taken back to Norway. The raiders did not care about books, only about the value of the gold that decorated them.

## SLAVS, BULGARS AND MAGYARS

In central Europe, groups of Slav tribes came from north-east Europe to settle in an area called the Balkans. Another Slav tribe, called the Bulgars, settled on the shores of the Black Sea. In about 900, nomads from Central Asia, called the Magyars, settled in present-day Hungary.

▲ This arch is part of the mosque at Cordoba, in southern Spain. The building was started by Emir Abd al-Rahman (ruled 756 to 788). He encouraged artists, scientists and scholars to come to this great city.

## MUSLIM POWER IN EUROPE

Since the early 700s Muslim soldiers from North Africa and Arabia had been attacking Europe. They conquered many Mediterranean islands and a large part of Spain. Muslim princes ruled over a brilliant multi-cultural civilization in southern Europe from their capital city at Cordoba, in southern Spain. In 732, at the Battle of Poitiers, they were stopped from advancing any further north into Europe by a Frankish army led by Charlemagne's grandfather.

## THE SPREAD OF ISLAM

MIDDLE EAST

The faith of Islam was taught by the Prophet Muhammad, who lived in Arabia from about 570 to 632. After he died, a new Muslim empire grew rapidly as Muslim preachers taught people about their faith, and Muslim soldiers conquered new territory in Arabia and the neighbouring lands. By 751 Muslim leaders, called caliphs, controlled a vast empire that stretched from the Chinese border to southern Spain. At first its capital city was at Damascus in Syria. Then in 762 Caliph al-Mansur founded a magnificent new city called Baghdad. It was laid out in a circular shape as a sign of the Muslim empire's unity and power.

▲ Muslim soldiers beseiging a Byzantine city on the Mediterranean island of Sicily, in 842. The Byzantines fought many battles against the Muslims for control of the Mediterranean Sea with its profitable trade routes and busy fishing fleets.

## THE BYZANTINE EMPIRE

MIDDLE EAST

There was another great power in the Middle East, called the Byzantine Empire. It was ruled from the old Roman city of Constantinople (present-day Istanbul), and covered present-day Greece and Turkey. The Byzantines were Christians, and they were often at war with their Muslim neighbours. The empire survived because it had the best navy in the world, and because Constantinople was surrounded by massive Roman walls. The Byzantines also had a special army called the Varangian Guard, made up of fierce soldiers recruited from Viking lands.

## RICH AND STRONG

AFRICA

North Africa was divided into many kingdoms, governed by Muslim rulers. They built fine new cities, like Kairouan (in present-day Tunisia), and encouraged trade, to the north across the Mediterranean Sea and to the south across the Sahara Desert. They kept strong armies, to conquer new lands. According to Muslim law, these rulers owed loyalty to the caliphs in Baghdad, but in fact they often ruled independently.

In north-east Africa, Christian kings ruled over the kingdoms of Nubia and Axum. They traded gold, ivory and slaves with rich Arabian ports across the Red Sea, and bought fine Indian cloth, perfumes and spices in return.

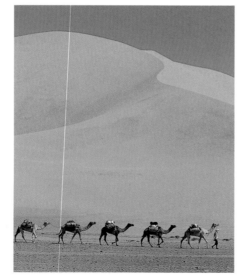

◄ A modern camel-train in the Sahara Desert. Berber merchants in Charlemagne's time travelled in this way along the trade routes that crossed the desert.

## BY CAMEL ACROSS THE DESERT

South of the Sahara, kingdoms like Ghana grew rich by trading with Berber merchants from North Africa. The Berbers took months to cross the long-distance routes across the Sahara, with caravans of up to a thousand camels. They carried copper (mined in the Sahara) and salt (made on the North African coast). The people of Ghana wanted copper to make tools. They used salt for cooking and for preserving food. In return they gave the Berbers gold, leather and slaves. Towns in Ghana such as Kumbi Saleh, which lay at the end of these trade routes, grew big and very busy. They were full of fine houses for merchants, and palaces where the royal family lived.

## HINDU KINGDOMS

**SOUTH ASIA**

In central and southern India there were several strong independent states. The Rashtrakuta dynasty of kings came to power in 750 and ruled until 973. They were Hindus, and built many temples as monuments to their faith and power. They often fought against the Chola dynasty, whose rulers became powerful in southern India around 800. The Chola rulers also built many temples. These were not just places of prayer. They were used as government offices, community centres, banks and schools.

## MUSLIMS IN INDIA

In the years before Charlemagne's reign, north India had been attacked by many invaders, including warlike tribes from Central Asia. Finally, in 712, Muslim soldiers won control of north-east India and set up new kingdoms there. Many Indian people did not like being ruled by invaders, but the years of peace that followed were good for craftworkers and traders, and helped the people become rich.

## KHMER EMPIRE

In about 700 the Khmer empire, based in present-day Cambodia, began to be an important power in South-east Asia. Khmer rulers conquered new lands, and captured many treasures and slaves. They used their wealth to build vast new cities, temples and palaces in present-day Cambodia and Vietnam. They also ruled land crossed by important trade routes between India and China.

► This temple at Ellora, in India, was built by kings of the Rashtrakuta dynasty. It was designed to look like mountain peaks, to represent the sacred mountain home of the Hindu god, Shiva.

## NEW IDEAS

For hundreds of years Japan had been ruled according to ancient traditions, based on the Shinto religion. This had shaped the law, art and government. But by about 700, new ideas from abroad were changing Japanese life. Most came from nearby China and Korea. They ranged from Buddhism, to new fashions in clothing, building and design. Japanese emperors reorganized their government so that officials worked in Chinese style, and their scribes began to use Chinese characters (signs used instead of letters) to write out Japanese words.

## NEW CITIES

Japanese emperors also built new cities in Chinese style. Between 710 and 794, they chose Nara, the site of a very famous Buddhist temple, to be the nation's capital. Then Emperor Kammu decided to build a new capital city at Kyoto. In the years that followed, Kyoto became filled with beautiful temples, palaces and monasteries in mixed Chinese-Japanese designs. This was because each new emperor built a new royal palace to live in, and new gardens and temples, too.

## THE TANG DYNASTY

In China the Tang emperors ruled from 618 to 907. They were famous for their skill at governing and their love of the arts. They supported artists and craftworkers and encouraged Chinese merchants to trade with people from many other lands. They also conquered new territories in the far west of China and in Central Asia. The Tang emperors built fine cities, such as Chang'an (see page 27), and encouraged foreign trading ships to call at busy Chinese ports, like Hangzhou.

▲ One of many fine temples built by Japanese emperors in their capital city of Kyoto. It was built during the Heian era, which lasted from 794 to 1185. Like many other important Japanese buildings, it is surrounded by beautiful gardens.

◄ Chinese artists of the Tang dynasty were famous for making works of art like this statue of a horse. It is made of pottery, and decorated with clay mouldings and a coloured glaze.

## HIDDEN BY TIME

Both North and South America were home to many different civilizations in Charlemagne's time. Because few kept written records, what we know about them can only be found out from remains such as tools, carvings, pottery or building materials. In the Arctic north, from about 800, people called the Dorset Inuit began to build bigger, better settlements than before. They made rough shelters from stone and earth, instead of animal skin tents. They also made more efficient harpoons and fishing spears. But all clues to their existence after about 1000 have been lost – no one knows for certain what happened to them.

► This small statue of a woman was found in the Arctic region of North America. It was carved from walrus-ivory by an Inuit artist who lived more than a thousand years ago, in about 700.

## PUEBLO FARMERS

Further south the Mogollon, Hohokam and Anasazi peoples managed to survive in semi-desert lands, living in settlements called pueblos. Their houses were like large blocks of flats, built in deep canyons, or half-underground, to shade themselves from the hot sun. They dug irrigation ditches to bring water to their crops.

▲ A wall-painting from the royal palace in the Mayan city of Bonampak. It shows musicians and dancers taking part in a ceremony in front of the king.

## MAYAN POWER

In Central America the Maya cleared land from the thick rainforest and built huge, pyramid-shaped temples and fine palaces. These cities were mainly religious centres, and only rulers, priests and nobles lived there. Ordinary people lived in nearby villages and farms. Mayan priests were skilled astronomers and also developed a way of writing using picture-symbols, called glyphs. Mayan cities were like independent states, but they traded goods such as pottery, chocolate, salt and slaves with one another.

## NEW SETTLERS

The Aboriginal people had lived in Australia for at least 50,000 years. But many other islands in the Pacific Ocean had never been inhabited, or had only been settled for a few hundred years. In Charlemagne's time, sailors and settlers were still discovering some of the most remote Pacific islands. Hawaii was first settled some time between 100 and 800, and New Zealand, from about 850 to 900.

# FAMOUS RULERS AND LEADERS

Charlemagne, like many rulers of his age, fought to defend his kingdom from invasion and to conquer new lands. Like other rulers he also saw himself as working for God, and gave money to pay for religious buildings and works of art. Rulers in Charlemagne's time were almost always men, although royal wives and mothers often gave important advice.

Communications between nations were slow and dangerous, but many rulers did make contact. Charlemagne and King Offa made trade agreements, and Indian kings sent messengers to Chinese leaders. The Muslim ruler Caliph Harun al-Rashid even sent Charlemagne an elephant as a present.

◀ This ornament is called the Alfred Jewel. It is probably the handle of a pointer, used like a finger to follow the words while reading a book. It was made out of gold and enamel for King Alfred the Great of Wessex, one of the few kings in Europe who could read and write.

### ALFRED THE GREAT

EUROPE

King Alfred the Great ruled the Anglo-Saxon kingdom of Wessex, in south-west England, from 871 to 899. Alfred spent most of his life fighting Viking invasions. He reorganized the English army and founded new fortress-towns. Unlike Charlemagne, Alfred was a skilful scholar. He wrote and translated several important religious books.

## KING OFFA

King Offa ruled an Anglo-Saxon kingdom in
the West Midlands of England, called Mercia,
from 757 to 796. He fought to unite several
small kingdoms into one large empire. He also
won new lands peacefully, by arranging marriages
for his daughters with neighbouring kings.
He defended Mercia from Welsh invasions by
building a huge wall made of wood and earth,
which is still called Offa's Dyke.

◀ A silver penny
made for King
Offa. Like
Charlemagne,
King Offa was
keen to increase
trade. He
produced new
high-quality
coins, to help
English merchants
trade across Europe.

▲ Caliph Harun al-Rashid is sitting
in the bath-house of his royal palace,
surrounded by servants. The walls and
floors are decorated with colourful tiles.
Towels are drying overhead. Cleanliness
was important to the Muslims. People
gave money to build public baths, and
merchants sold lotions and perfumes,
scented with flowers, spices and herbs.

## BANDITS AND KINGS

Scandinavia and other Viking lands were ruled by
strong, warlike kings. King Harald Fairhair, who
lived from about 865 to 945, was the first ruler to
unite Norway into a single kingdom. He also sent
Viking raiders to attack and settle in Scotland,
Ireland and Iceland, and encouraged Viking trade.

There were also many wild, lawless leaders
of Viking warrior bands, who led their men far
from home on pirate raids for months or years
at a time. One such warrior was Ragnar, who
led his Vikings to attack and conquer the city of
Paris, France, in 845. They demanded a ransom of
more than 3000 kilograms of silver from Charles
the Bald, the French king, and stole iron bars
from the city gates as souvenirs.

## CALIPH OF BAGHDAD

**MIDDLE EAST**

Caliph Harun al-Rashid ruled the Muslim lands
in the Middle East from 786 to 809. As Caliph, he
had a duty to defend the Islamic faith, as well as
govern his lands. He won praise as a warrior,
fighting against the Byzantines, and putting down
revolts on the borders of his empire. He was also
famous for making the city of Baghdad (see page
25) rich and famous. Harun's favourite wife,
Zubaydah, encouraged scholarship and the arts,
and set up many Muslim charities.

## BYZANTINE EMPRESS

Empress Irene was the first woman to rule the Byzantine Empire. She came from a poor Greek family, but she was beautiful, clever and ambitious. Emperor Leo IV fell in love, and married her in 769. After he died in 780 she took over power. Her son Constantine VI should have been the next emperor, but Irene put him in prison and blinded him, along with her dead husband's five brothers. There were also rumours that she wanted to marry Charlemagne. This alarmed the Byzantine army and in 802 they shut her up in a convent, where she died a year later.

► No portraits of Empress Irene have survived, but this mosaic, made soon after Irene died, gives us some idea of how she might have dressed. The woman on the right is a saint, but she is shown as a Byzantine noblewoman. She is wearing a jewelled crown, bracelets, necklaces and earrings, and her gold-coloured silk robe is decorated with beautiful embroidery.

▲ The courtyard of the huge and splendid mosque Governor Ibn Tulun built at Fustat, in Egypt. It was built in just three years, between 876 and 879.

## SOLDIER AND PHILOSOPHER

Ahmad Ibn Tulun was one of the most famous Muslim rulers of North African lands. He was born in Baghdad, where he studied philosophy at university, and trained as a soldier. His father was a Turkish slave who served as a senior soldier in the army. When his father died, young Ibn Tulun took over his army duties.

In 868 Ibn Tulun was sent to Egypt. There he put down local rebellions, reformed the government, and won the loyalty of the army – all in two years. As Governor of Egypt he built a fine new capital city at Fustat, with a royal palace, gardens, a racecourse, a sports ground, a free hospital and homes for his wives, officials, and servants. He built a mosque there, too. Then he set out to conquer new lands in the Middle East. He died in 883, from an illness caught on campaign.

## RICHEST RULERS IN THE WORLD

We know about Ibn Tulun because Muslim rulers hired scribes to keep written records of what was happening. We know less about rulers in other parts of Africa, because they did not use writing. People passed on their history in songs and stories. These stories show that the kings of Ghana were among the richest men in the world in Charlemagne's time, and that their wealth came from huge gold mines. They employed many advisors to help them rule, and to collect taxes from trade with other countries.

Tombs of West African rulers have been discovered, full of objects made of bronze, ivory and gold. These treasures show how rich and powerful many African kings were.

◄ This bronze head is one of many treasures found in a royal tomb at Igbo-Ukwu, in West Africa. The man is wearing a headdress, and his face is marked with a pattern of scars – often a sign of high rank.

## A HINDU DYNASTY

**SOUTH ASIA**

In India the Rashtrakuta kings invited artists and scholars to the court. Krishna I, who ruled from about 756 to 774, paid for many works of art, and had a temple cut out of rock at Ellora (see page 15). Krishna also encouraged craftwork and trade. Ships sailed from his kingdom to the rich islands of Java and Sumatra and beyond.

## EARLY TOURISM

In Sumatra, the rulers of the Srivijaya empire grew rich by demanding taxes from merchant ships arriving from Arabia, southern India and China. After about 700 Sumatra became a centre for pilgrims visiting Buddhist scholars and holy shrines. The emperors made money from this growing pilgrim tourist trade.

► This stone carving is part of a temple at Borobudur, in Java (also see page 39). It was built in about 800 by Buddhist rulers there. The carving shows a sailing ship fitted with outriggers – planks joined to the hull, to keep the ship stable at sea. Ships like this carried traders and religious teachers between countries such as India, Java and Sumatra.

► The remains of the Hindu temple of Preah Koh are close to the Khmer capital city of Angkor. The temple was built by Emperor Indravarman I, who ruled from 877 to 889. Like other Khmer rulers, Indravarman was honoured as a god, but he still worshipped the ancient Hindu gods.

## GOD-KINGS

SOUTH ASIA

In 802 the Khmer ruler Jayavarman II moved the capital of the Khmer empire to a mountain near Angkor and declared that he was a god-king. He claimed that his power came from the Hindu god Shiva. From then on all Khmer rulers were seen as gods. They organized people to work hard to grow food, weave cloth and make beautiful jewels to please the royal family and all the priests and courtiers who lived in the palaces with them.

## THE SHINING EMPEROR

EAST ASIA

In China the Tang emperors led a series of conquests, taking over new territories from Afghanistan to Korea and Tibet. The emperors made strict new laws to help them run their huge empire, and employed large numbers of officials to carry them out. To become officials, people had to pass very difficult exams.

Tang Xuanzong, who reigned from 712 to 756, was one of the most famous emperors. He was known as the Shining Emperor, because of his brilliant achievements. He defended China against enemy attacks from Central Asia and built new towns. He welcomed foreign merchants and travelling scholars, encouraged new inventions, and gave money to painters, poets and musicians to produce wonderful works of art.

◄ Part of a painted scroll showing Chinese Emperor Tang Xuanzong with two servants. The emperor is ready to go hunting, with bow and arrows. The man on the left is holding his red-painted bow.

◀ Part of a stone doorway, carved in about 725. It shows a Mayan king called Shield Jaguar (left) and his wife. The king is putting on special clothes, headdress and jewels, to go to war. His wife is holding a mask, which the king will wear later to cover his face.

## MYTHS AND LEGENDS

Other South American peoples recorded the names of their kings in myths and legends. In the far north of Peru, the Sican people told tales of King Naymlap who arrived to take over their kingdom in a balsa-wood raft. The Chimu people who lived nearby, told stories of King Tacaynamo. They believed he had founded their capital city, called Chan Chan.

## SETTLERS AND SAILORS

**AUSTRALASIA**

We know even fewer names of rulers who lived in Australasia in Charlemagne's time. But we do know, from later travellers' tales, that the people who settled in New Zealand and Easter Island belonged to several different tribes, each ruled by a chief. These chiefs were fighters and war-leaders. Leaders of these Pacific island settlers must also have been responsible for navigating on long sea voyages, organizing the settlers, and planning the layout of farms and villages in their new homeland.

## MAYAN RULERS

**AMERICAS**

We do not know the names of many rulers in the Americas in Charlemagne's time, because most peoples did not keep written records. But a few, like the Maya, did keep lists of rulers. From these we know that Mayan kings were served by nobles, priests and warriors. Each ruler tried to construct the richest buildings to outdo rivals in other cities. They even fought one another to show who was more powerful. Lord Pacal, who died in 683, made his city of Palenque (see page 35) one of the richest Mayan settlements. In Charlemagne's time some of the greatest Mayan kings lived there. They paid for massive stone temples and palaces to be built at Palenque. These were decorated with picture-histories carved in the stone walls.

▶ An Easter Island chief once owned this command-stick (called an 'ua'). It is made of polished wood, and carved with two male faces, looking backwards and forwards – perhaps as a sign of the chief's superhuman power.

# HOW PEOPLE LIVED

All around the world, there were many contrasts in the way people lived in Charlemagne's time. In many lands there was a small powerful group of warriors or priests, linked to a rich court, with rulers who rewarded their followers. The rest of the population often struggled to survive. Most people lived in simple homes in the country, and worked on the land. But there were also cities, where rulers, merchants, lawyers, doctors and money-lenders lived. Craftworkers, innkeepers, and entertainers made their homes in cities, too. The biggest cities were full of palaces, religious buildings and markets. In China, and Muslim countries, some cities had sports centres, theatres, clean running water, libraries and hospitals, too.

▼ An Anglo-Saxon farmer in England steering a heavy ox-drawn plough. In most of Europe, ordinary men, women and children worked hard on the land. They gave the estate owners a share of the food they produced, and sometimes money as well, in return for cottages to live in, and small plots of farmland. They wore rough homespun clothes, and ate simple food, such as vegetable soup and bread.

## OWNING THE LAND

European kings gave large areas of land, called estates, to loyal nobles and army leaders who helped them rule. They also gave estates to bishops and to the pope. The sale of meat, crops, wool, wine and wood from these estates made the landowners rich. They lived in big houses with servants, ate good food and wore fine woollen robes, trimmed with fur and jewels.

## VIKING FOOD

In Scandinavia, where the weather was cold, few crops grew well. So Viking families caught fish, seals and walrus from the sea, and climbed cliffs to collect sea-birds' eggs. They also kept sheep, goats and cows for meat and milk, gathered wild herbs, nuts and berries, and hunted bears and deer in the dark pinewoods.

◄ The Vikings wore brooches to fasten their clothes. This gold brooch was made for a rich woman by a Viking craftworker.

## HOME LIFE

Vikings built houses of wood and stone, with thatched roofs to keep out the cold. In places like Iceland, where few trees grew, they made walls from stone and slabs of turf, with more turf on the roof. Most houses had no windows, to keep out draughts, and for extra warmth a big fire was kept burning all year round.

► Baghdad, the capital city of the caliphs, rulers of the Muslim world.

## A NEW CITY

Baghdad was still a new city in Charlemagne's time, but already it was one of the largest and richest cities in the world. It was surrounded by a strong wall built of mud brick and guarded by four huge gates. The caliph's palace was in the centre, surrounded by gardens and high walls. Mosques, army barracks and government offices stood nearby. Thousands of ordinary people, such as scribes, street-cleaners, craftworkers, librarians, shopkeepers, fruitsellers, schoolteachers, water-carriers and bath-house keepers, lived and worked in an outer ring of city buildings and in settlements outside the city walls. Like many cities, Baghdad had problems with riots, muggings and gangs roaming the streets.

## ALMONDS AND APRICOTS

Farmers in the Middle East herded sheep and goats, and grew crops such as olives, barley, onions, marrows and aubergines. They lived in villages of stone and mud-brick houses, and planted orchards of almond and apricot trees. Where there was enough water, in river valleys or irrigated fields, they grew grapes and planted sugar cane.

## COOL CLOTHES

**AFRICA**

In North Africa people wore long, loose clothes, which allowed air to flow round their bodies to keep them cool. Rich people also wore silk, brought from China. In the desert, herdsmen and merchants wore veils to protect their faces from sand blown by the wind.

## RAINFORESTS AND GRASSLANDS

In the rainforests of Central Africa, hunters and farmers killed deer, snakes and crocodiles with bows and arrows or spears. They planted yams, plantains and oil-palms in fields cleared among the forest trees. They lived in houses with mud walls, grass roofs and shady courtyards. Floors were covered with mats woven from dried leaves and grass. Houses belonging to the richest villagers might also have carved wooden doors.

Further south villagers kept cattle, and grew crops of millet and sorghum. Women pounded these grains in big wooden bowls, then cooked them with water to make thick porridge.

## TRADE AND MARKET TOWNS

All across northern Africa, people made their living by trade. As well as a few big cities, there were many market towns. Traders there bought and sold local produce, such as meat, animal skins, vegetables and grain. They also traded goods made by local craftworkers, who were famous for metalwork, jewellery, basket-making, leather goods and coloured cloths.

Town houses were built close together. They were flat-roofed and made of bricks of mud that had been baked in the sun. Rulers, nobles and rich merchants could afford houses with many rooms, shady courtyards and perhaps even a cooling fountain or pool.

▼ These buildings in a village in north-west Africa are built in a style that has changed little over hundreds of years. The houses are made of sun-dried mud on a wooden frame, with a straw roof. Grain-stores are raised above the ground on rocks, to stop rats and insects stealing the grain.

▲ Indian elephants were used by villagers to carry heavy loads, and to hunt wild boar and tigers in the forest. They could also be trained to fight in battle. These elephants were carved in about 800 on a Hindu temple in southern India.

## INDIAN VILLAGES

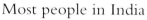
**SOUTH ASIA**

Most people in India lived in villages and worked on farms. They built simple houses out of stone, wood and mud, thatched with straw or palm-leaves. In the hot, rainy south people grew rice, and gathered mangoes and coconuts. Some villagers grew cash crops, such as pepper, spices, cotton, and sweet-smelling sandalwood, to sell in towns. In the cooler north they grew wheat and chickpeas. Villagers also kept goats, chickens, and cows to supply milk and dung, which could be burned as fuel. Water-buffalo pulled ploughs, and turned water-wheels. These used buckets to lift water from rivers to irrigate the land.

In southern India, Burma and Sri Lanka, many people worked as miners, searching for rubies and sapphires. These were treasured worldwide. Most European kings, including Charlemagne, probably had at least one precious stone in their crowns, brought all the way from India.

## SILK, PERFUMES AND JEWELS

**EAST ASIA**

Chang'an, the capital of China, was the biggest city in the world. More than a million people lived there. It had wide streets, huge markets and royal gardens. Traders from many lands travelled to Chang'an bringing perfumes from Arabia, furs from Siberia, and jewels and spices from India. In return they bought tea, paper, porcelain and precious Chinese silk. Many foreign merchants and scholars also made their home in Chang'an.

Rich people in Chang'an, including merchants and government officials, lived in large wooden houses filled with fine pottery, jade and paintings. They wore long silk robes, dyed in glowing colours. They invited one another to feasts and concerts of music and poetry, and played games like chess and cards. Polo was also a fashionable sport, played by the Emperor Xuanzong himself.

► A pottery model of a camel loaded with goods. It was made in Tang China in about 700. Merchants travelling to and from rich Chinese cities carried their valuable trade goods by camel.

EAST ASIA

## LIVING IN THE CLOUDS

In Japan, the emperor and his courtiers living in the city of Kyoto were surrounded by palaces, temples and beautiful gardens. They wore clothes made of silk, and spent the time painting, and writing and listening to poetry and music. They had no contact with ordinary people in the outside world, so they became known as 'the people who lived in the clouds'.

◄ This statue of a lady holding a flower was made by craftworkers in Tang China. Her flowing robe and high headdress show us what rich people were wearing in Chang'an (see page 27). Japanese courtiers also liked to wear the latest fashions from China.

## WORKING LIVES

Ordinary Japanese people worked hard all year round, growing crops of rice, wheat and millet to feed their families and to pay taxes to their landowners. They also worked as labourers and craftworkers, helping to build new towns, and creating beautiful clothes, pottery, woodwork and gardens for the emperor and his nobles to enjoy.

Because there are many earthquakes in Japan, all Japanese buildings, from royal palaces to farmers' huts, were built of wood, with paper screens instead of inside walls. Wooden buildings were less likely to crush people inside if they collapsed during a quake.

## LOCAL LIFESTYLES

AMERICAS

In North America how people lived depended on their environment. They had to build their homes, make their clothes and find their food from local soil, water, plants and animals. In the frozen Arctic north, the Inuit people hunted walrus and built winter shelters, called igloos, out of blocks of snow.

On the north-east coast the Algonquian people hunted deer and beaver in the woods, and grew crops of maize, beans and pumpkins. They built houses out of wooden poles, which they covered with tree-bark. In the warm, dry south-west, the Hohokam and Anasazi people built their homes out of sun-dried mud brick. They also used clay to make beautiful pottery bowls, dishes and storage jars.

▼ Men and women taking part in a ceremonial dance, painted on a pot made by craftworkers from the Hohokam people of south-west North America.

## MISSISSIPPI MOUND BUILDERS

In the warm, wet Mississippi valley, farmers grew so much maize that the population began to increase. After about 700 they began to build cities as centres of trade and religion. One of the largest of these was called Cahokia. Important buildings, such as temples and nobles' houses, were built on flat-topped mounds of earth.

## RAINFOREST LIFE

In Mayan cities ordinary people worked as craftworkers or as market traders. Others became warriors or royal servants. But most Mayan people were farmers. They worked outside the city, clearing fields from the rainforest using slash and burn techniques. They grew crops of maize, cacao and pineapples, and hunted lizards, jaguars and wild birds in the rainforest.

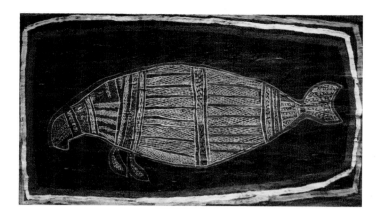

▲ A sea-cow painted on bark by an Aboriginal artist in the far north of Australia. Aboriginal hunters and fishermen used nets and spears to catch many kinds of fish, as well as large sea-mammals like these.

▼ This plump Mayan merchant looks wealthy and well-fed. His portrait was painted on a pot by a Mayan craftworker.

## ABORIGINAL HUNTERS

AUSTRALASIA

In Australia Aboriginal peoples lived as hunters and gatherers, spearing kangaroo, emu, possum, snakes and lizards, or trapping them in nets. They dug up edible roots and grubs, looked for birds' eggs, and collected wild grass seeds, berries and nuts. At night they lit campfires and made shelters out of branches or animal skins.

## SETTLING IN NEW ZEALAND

Settlers in New Zealand probably brought with them seeds of plants they used to grow in their original island homes. But because the climate in New Zealand was colder and wetter, they found the only crop that grew well was sweet potatoes.

So they had to adapt to the new environment. They looked for new sources of food by hunting, gathering and fishing. Along the southern coast there were seals, shellfish and whales. Further inland they found large, flightless birds, including the moa. These birds had no natural enemies until humans arrived. The settlers found them easy to kill, because they had not learned to be afraid, or to protect themselves.

# DISCOVERY AND INVENTION

The wars and invasions that took place in many parts of the world between 700 and 900 meant that it was not always a good time for quiet study. But in some ways, fighting and migrations did help technology to develop. For example, Viking sailors designed fast, seaworthy ships to help them make raids into new lands. Conquests also spread knowledge from one country to another. In this way Frankish warriors learned about stirrups, which made it easier to fight on horseback, from Central Asian nomads who attacked Europe from the east.

## FARMING

**EUROPE**

In Charlemagne's time, the population of Europe was increasing. More food was needed to feed the extra people, so scrubland and woodland were cleared for new farms. In northern Europe, where the weather was wet and the soil heavy, farmers used strong wooden ploughs to prepare the soil for planting seeds (see page 24). From about 900, plough blades were tipped with iron to make them even stronger. In southern Europe, where the weather was hot and dry, huge waterwheels were built to raise water from rivers to irrigate fields.

▲ A copper astrolabe made by Ahmad ibn Khalif, a Muslim scientist who lived in Iraq in the 800s. Astrolabes helped sailors work out their position at sea by measuring the height of the sun above the horizon. The higher it was at midday, the closer the ship was to the Equator.

## VIKING SHIPS

Some of the most important inventions in Europe were made by Viking boatbuilders, to help them cross stormy northern seas to make raids on new lands. Everything about a Viking ship was carefully designed. Its wooden hull was light and shallow, so it could skim over the surface of the waves. Its flat bottom meant that it could be sailed right up on to a beach to land. It had a large square sail, to catch the wind, but also oars to row it through water in sheltered bays, or when there was no wind. Turning vanes, fitted to the mast, helped Viking sailors make the best use of wind power. Flaps covered the oar holes in the hull, so that water would not get in.

## FINDING THE WAY

Viking sailors had no maps. Instead, they used bearing dials, like portable sun dials, and magnetic lodestones to plot their course when out of sight of land. They also learned to understand the flight of birds, the movement of shoals of fish, wave patterns, shallow water currents, and even earthy smells, such as the smell of sheep, to tell them when they were approaching land.

## ENCOURAGING LEARNING

**MIDDLE EAST**

Muslim rulers encouraged scholars, scientists and inventors to work in their lands. They gave money to build libraries, universities, hospitals and schools. Muslim scholars were famous for their knowledge of mathematics, astronomy, building design and medicine, especially herbal medicines. Scientists also invented and improved instruments, such as the astrolabe, to help sailors steer a straight course at sea.

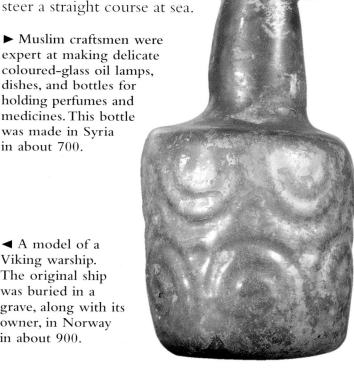

► **Muslim craftsmen were expert at making delicate coloured-glass oil lamps, dishes, and bottles for holding perfumes and medicines. This bottle was made in Syria in about 700.**

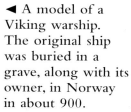

◄ **A model of a Viking warship. The original ship was buried in a grave, along with its owner, in Norway in about 900.**

## HANDING DOWN KNOWLEDGE

Muslim scholars copied and translated manuscripts of inventions and discoveries made long ago. Among the most important were writings by two scientists from Ancient Greece: Aristotle and Ptolemy. If Middle Eastern scholars had not translated their works on biology, medicine and astronomy, they might have been lost for ever.

## DOMES AND SUNDIALS

AFRICA

For Muslims, domed roofs had a religious meaning – they reminded people of heaven. But it was very difficult to build a domed roof on top of a square or rectangular building. Byzantine architects were the first to achieve this, in the 500s. In Charlemagne's time, Muslim architects in North Africa and the Middle East copied and improved this technology. They built many mosques with high domed roofs, such as the Great Mosque at Kairouan (see page 38). Muslim builders also liked to include other examples of technology in their designs, such as sun dials and fountains.

## IRON AND BRONZE

In Charlemagne's time African craftworkers had become famous for their skill at metalworking, using ancient techniques. They cast delicate sculptures from brass and bronze, like the one below. They also smelted iron by heating crushed iron ore in special dome-shaped ovens. They heated the ovens with charcoal. This was because they discovered that charcoal fires burned at a hotter temperature than fires of wood, and so melted metal better. The iron in the ore melted and separated from the rock. It could then be heated again, and hammered into weapons and farm tools.

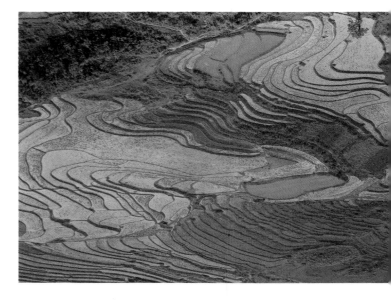

▲ Rice growing in present-day Vietnam. Khmer farmers in Charlemagne's time grew rice in flooded fields like these.

## WATER ENGINEERS

SOUTH ASIA

In present-day Cambodia and Vietnam, the main source of food for most people was rice. Rice needs warm weather and a steady supply of water to grow well. Too much or too little water means a poor harvest. To make sure that there was always the right amount of water available, Khmer rulers gave orders for huge reservoirs, called barays, to be dug. Barays collected the heavy monsoon rainfall that fell in the summer, so it could be used all year round. Khmer kings also planned clever irrigation schemes to control the flow of water into the rice fields, so that they never became too wet or too dry.

◄ This bronze container was made by skilled African craftworkers in Igbo Ukwu in the 800s. It is shaped like a shell, with a figure of a leopard on top.

► This statue of the Hindu god Shiva was made in southern India when the Chola dynasty was in power. Worshippers prayed to Shiva to give them good health and many children. They believed Shiva had power to cure disease. He was also honoured as the guardian god of healing herbs.

## HERBS AND PRAYERS

There had been skilful doctors in India for thousands of years. Often, they worked side by side with Hindu priests to try and cure disease. They used ancient herbal remedies, as well as religious ceremonies and prayers. From about 700 the Kalamukas, a religious group in southern India, made a special effort to continue the traditions of ancient Hindu sciences. They built temples and monasteries where they worshipped the god Shiva, lord of long life and medicine.

## MATHS AND ETERNITY

Indian mathematicians were famous for their skill. For hundreds of years they had worked with huge numbers, trying to measure not just our time, but also eternity. Without computers to help, it was easy to make mistakes in their calculations. So by about 200 BC, Indian scholars had invented two mathematical tools – special signs for the numbers one to nine, and the figure zero, to help them do more accurate sums.

## MUSLIM STUDENTS

Indian mathematical skills were not widely known outside India, but in Charlemagne's time, students came from many lands to study in Indian colleges. By about 800, Muslim scholars had copied out many Indian mathematical ideas into Arabic. They began to use the figure zero and the signs for numbers to help them work more accurately with huge numbers. This knowledge did not reach Europe until hundreds of years later, but is now used all around the world.

## PORCELAIN AND POTTERY

**EAST ASIA**

Chinese people had been making pottery for thousands of years, but they were continually trying out new materials, techniques, and designs. During the Tang era, Chinese potters perfected a type of very fine pottery, known as porcelain. It was made from a special white clay, called kaolin, and was fired at high temperatures, until it became hard, glassy and smooth.

At the same time, Chinese potters also invented brightly-coloured glazes, which they used to decorate little statues like the ones you can see on pages 28 and 40. A single statue might have four different glazes, each carefully made from powdered chemicals mixed with clay. After about 900, the potters stopped making these figures. Their knowledge was forgotten, and not discovered again for over a thousand years.

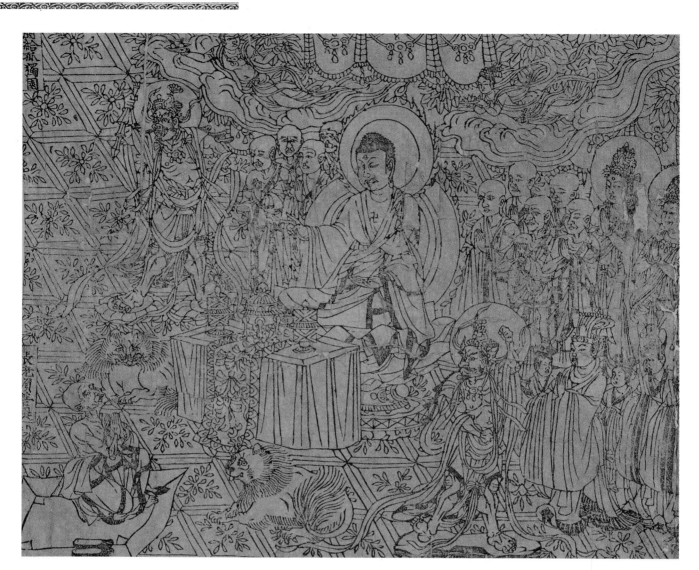

## PAPER, PRINTING AND BOOKS

EAST ASIA

Paper was invented in China in about 100 AD, but the process was kept a secret for more than 600 years. In the 600s and 700s, the knowledge of paper-making spread first to Japan, probably taken by Buddhist monks, and then west via the busy trading city of Samarkand.

The first wood-block prints were also made in China, between 704 and 751. The design, which could be a picture or writing, was carved on to a small block of wood. To make the print, the block was rubbed with ink, and a piece of paper was pressed on top. By the 800s Chinese craftworkers were producing books by printing one page after another on long paper scrolls.

▲ *The Diamond Sutra*, the world's oldest-known printed book, was made in 868. Sutras are collections of Buddhist holy writings. This page shows a Buddhist worshipper (in the bottom left-hand corner) kneeling in prayer in front of an altar.

## TICKING CLOCKS

Chinese scientists invented a water-driven clock with a mechanism called a ratchet. The ratchet, which was like a toothed wheel with a lever, allowed time to be measured in a regular series of jerks, rather than in continuous uncontrolled flow. This caused the clock to make a ticking sound and is now called clockwork. It was far more accurate than any clock invented before.

## CROPS FROM THE DESERT

AMERICAS

Native American peoples, like the Hohokam and Anasazi, who lived in south-west North America, had to find ways of surviving in dry desert land. They dug wide trenches to carry water from distant mountains all the way to their fields. By carefully managing the flow of water, they could grow two crops every year. The first was in spring, when the mountain snows melted. The second was in late summer, when rain fell on the mountain slopes.

## MAYAN MATHS

Mayan priests were skilled mathematicians and astronomers, and all important Mayan cities had an observatory. Mayan scribes used three basic symbols for their calculations: a dot for one, a bar for five and a shell for zero. They used these mostly for measuring time. The Mayans had five different calendars, although they only used two on a daily basis. One, used by farmers, was based on the movements of the sun. The other was used by priests to calculate religious festival days. Historians now know that the Mayan calendars were more accurate than the one used in Europe by Charlemagne and his scribes.

## OCEAN-GOING CANOES

AUSTRALASIA

Pacific islanders sailed thousands of kilometres – further than anyone else dared travel by sea at the time – in wooden dug-out canoes. The canoes were carved out of single tree-trunks with tools of bone, stone, sharp shells and whale ivory. The canoes were fitted with wooden frames on either side of the hull, which helped them stay upright on the huge ocean waves.

## FISHING WITH KITES

The Pacific islanders also went deep-sea fishing in their canoes, and invented kites to help them. By attaching a fishing line and hooks to the kite, they could throw a fishing line so that the kite carried it many kilometres away. This meant that fish were not frightened by any noise or shadows made by the sailors. It also allowed sailors to catch fish in dangerous waters where they could not sail, for example close to underwater coral reefs.

► These are the ruins of the royal palace in the Mayan city of Palenque. The tower was built around 700 by King Kan-Xul II, the younger brother of Lord Pacal (see page 23). It was built as an observatory where astronomers and priests could study the stars.

# THE CREATIVE WORLD

▲ In Charlemagne's time, manuscripts were written out by hand, and decorated with glowing pictures. Such beautiful pages were often given special covers. This book cover is made of silver, covered with a thin layer of gold, and has been inlaid with precious stones. It was made in France around 800. In the centre, there is a carved ivory panel showing Jesus on the Cross.

In Charlemagne's time painters, sculptors, builders, metalworkers, potters and jewellers created many lovely works of art. They used precious materials, such as gold, silver, ivory, silk, crystal and precious stones, and used slow, careful techniques that took many years to learn. Everything was made by hand – from huge Mayan temples to the tiniest illustration in a Christian or Muslim holy book.

Most ordinary people could not afford to own art treasures like these. They were usually made to honour different gods or religious leaders, or to bring glory to noble families and powerful kings.

## COPYING FROM THE PAST

EUROPE

Many of the carvings and other artworks made in Charlemagne's time used traditional Christian symbols, such as angels, or the Cross on which Jesus was crucified. But Charlemagne also wanted to recreate the glory of the Roman Empire in his own lands. So he told his architects and craftworkers to study the remains of old Roman paintings, statues and buildings and to use typical Roman features, such as flowing robes, tall columns and rounded arches, in their own work.

▲ A fragment of silk cloth, made by Byzantine craftworkers. It is woven with a pattern of heroes fighting with lions.

## NEW IDEAS

Charlemagne liked his workers to try out new building designs. He asked a monk called Odo of Metz to design a new palace for him at Aachen. Its chapel had a huge entrance and tall towers to impress visitors.

Many monks spent their lives copying out Christian manuscripts. They painted pictures in the margins to illustrate them, using bright colours and lively designs. Rich people paid for manuscripts and gave them to churches and monasteries, sometimes as a penance, sometimes to show off their generosity and importance.

## NORTH AND SOUTH

In southern Europe, Spanish craftworkers often mixed Muslim and Christian designs in their buildings. They were especially clever at making objects in metal, inlaid with jewels. In northern Europe Celtic monks produced beautiful manuscripts and stone carvings in a dramatic, swirling style. In Viking Scandinavia there were no churches or religious manuscripts, but people carved fine tombstones, and made beautiful metalwork and rich jewels.

## RELIGIOUS ART

  MIDDLE EAST

In Muslim lands, many mosques, colleges and libraries were built in Charlemagne's time, and the greatest works of art were often for religious use. But Middle Eastern craftworkers in Muslim and Byzantine countries also made lovely objects to decorate the homes of rich people. They made glass and crystal lamps, pottery bowls and tiles, and wove fine wool carpets and brightly-coloured silks.

## HOLY PICTURES

Constantinople was full of beautiful churches, paid for by Byzantine rulers. Churches were decorated with wall-paintings and mosaics in beautiful colours, silver and gold. Painters also made religious pictures, called icons. Many people believed icons had special powers to protect them, and hung them in their churches and in their homes.

◄ A page from *The Book of Kells*, a manuscript copy of the Gospels (from the Bible). It was made in about 800 by Irish monks, probably working in Scotland. They have used Celtic, Saxon and northern English designs.

## HOLY WORDS

The text of the Qur'an, the Muslim holy book, was first written down during the 600s. The earliest writers used lots of different ways of writing and spelling, which some readers found hard to understand. So in about 900, scholars produced a standard version of the text, using the most precise forms of writing and spelling. This is still used today.

To show their faith and skill, Muslim scribes in North Africa and the Middle East copied out the words of the Qur'an in beautiful flowing calligraphy, and decorated each page with coloured inks or pure gold. The Muslim faith taught artists not to show people or any living creature in their work, because only God can create life. So artists decorated their manuscripts and buildings with geometric patterns, or plant and flower designs.

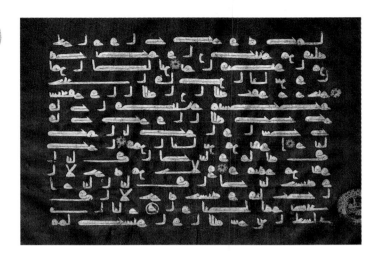

▲ A page from a copy of the Qur'an, made in North Africa around 800. The scribes have used Kufic script, which is made up of straight lines and sharp angles. This made it suitable for carving on stone. Many mosques were decorated with carved words from the Qur'an.

## AFRICAN MOSQUES

In North Africa Muslim rulers built many mosques. One of the first was the Great Mosque at Kairouan in Tunisia. Each local ruler wanted his mosque to be the finest, so the best craftworkers were brought in from all over the Muslim world. This was partly to show respect for Allah (the Arab word for God), and partly to show how rich and holy the rulers were. When Ibn Tulun (see page 20) built his mosque at Fustat in 879, he brought craftworkers all the way from Iraq so they could use the latest designs. Smaller African mosques were often built using local building techniques and in local styles.

◄ The Great Mosque at Kairouan, in present-day Tunisia, built in 836. It has a domed roof and a sundial in the courtyard. For Muslim architects, religion, art and technology were all part of the same knowledge.

## BRONZE, COPPER AND GOLD

In West Africa metalworkers in Igbo Ukwu created lifelike bronze statues of people and animals. They also decorated everyday metal items, such as pots, bowls and sword handles, with elaborate patterns. Metalworkers from the Berber people also made beautiful jewellery from copper and gold.

## STONE TEMPLES

**SOUTH ASIA**

In the 700s and 800s many temples were built in South Asian lands, especially in India, Cambodia, and on the island of Java. They were all built by rich and powerful kings, and were very big, very grand, and richly decorated with stone carvings and statues. Many of the carvings show ancient religious myths and legends in a series of panels, almost like a comic strip. The artists often included carved portraits of past and present kings.

## WOODEN PALACES

Temples were made of stone, which is why their ruins are still standing. Some palaces, especially in Cambodia, were also made of stone. But many royal palaces were made of wood, and decayed hundreds of years ago. From descriptions written at the time, we know that the palaces were as magnificent as the temples, and built by the same expert craftworkers for the glory of their kings. Inside, the rooms were decorated with silk cushions and carpets. There were carved wooden doors and screens that separated the royal family from the public gaze.

▼ The Buddhist temple at Borobudur, on the island of Java (see also page 21). It was built of black volcanic stone in about 800, and is shaped like a huge pyramid. Each side of the pyramid is covered with carvings telling the story of the Buddha, and showing scenes from everyday life.

## THE SILK ROAD

**EAST ASIA**

In China craftworkers made fine porcelain dishes, lifelike pottery statues and delicate silk cloth. These were sold to rich customers at home and in faraway lands. Merchants carried luxury goods along a network of tracks called the Silk Road, which ran from China to busy trading cities in Europe and the Middle East.

In many parts of China, and in towns along the Silk Road, rich people's tombs were decorated with wall-paintings showing the dead person, their family and friends in happy scenes from everyday life. Fierce-looking pottery statues also stood at the entrance to many tombs, to protect the dead people inside from demons and ghosts.

▶ This pottery statue of a tomb-guardian was made in China, in about 700. The guardian is trampling a demon spirit underfoot to protect the dead people buried in the tomb. The statue is decorated with a brightly-coloured glaze.

## A GOLDEN AGE

Chinese people enjoyed watching dancing and listening to music and poems. The years when the Tang dynasty ruled (618 to 907) are often called the Golden Age of Chinese poetry. More than 48,000 poems have survived from that time. Chinese scholars believed that poetry-writing was the highest form of art, so all keen young students learned how to write verses. Poetry-writing even became part of the exams taken by men who wished to become top government officials. Works by the most famous Tang poets, such as Li Bo, remained popular for hundreds of years.

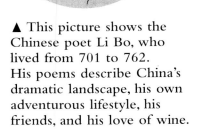

▲ This picture shows the Chinese poet Li Bo, who lived from 701 to 762. His poems describe China's dramatic landscape, his own adventurous lifestyle, his friends, and his love of wine.

## USING LOCAL MATERIALS

AMERICAS

Many different types of arts and crafts were created in America. Size, shape, decoration and design all varied with local materials and customs. In the Arctic north, the Inuit people made delicate carvings of animals from walrus ivory and soft soapstone. In the north-western forests, craftworkers made totem poles from tree-trunks. In the dry south-west of North America, potters shaped clay into dishes and bowls, and decorated them with dramatic designs.

Further south, the Maya decorated temples and palaces with brightly-coloured wall-paintings, showing festivals and scenes from palace life. In present-day Peru, Huari artists made mosaics and jewellery out of precious stones and shells.

◄ A disk made from turquoise (a semi-precious stone) and shell. It is one of a pair, which were probably worn as earrings. The Huari craftworker has used great skill to fit tiny chips of stone and shell together in a dramatic design.

## CLOSE TO THE SEA

AUSTRALASIA

Most Pacific islanders spent their lives close to the sea, and this was shown in their art. They used sea materials, such as coloured shells, mother-of-pearl, coral and sharks' teeth, to make jewellery and to decorate statues of their spirits and gods.

## MAPS IN WORDS

In Australia Aboriginal artists, singers and storytellers created images and recorded the adventures of magical figures from the Dreamtime. This was a time, long ago, when the Ancestors of people, plants and animals created the world. Traditional stories often had a useful purpose, too, and could be used as 'maps in words'. For example, details from a traditional tale of a hero chasing a kangaroo across a lonely landscape could be used to help wandering hunters remember the right tracks to take to rock-shelters and water-holes.

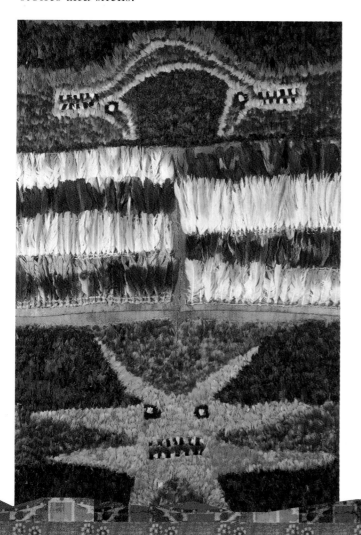

◄ A tunic made by the Huari people, some time between 700 and 1000. It is woven from feathers plucked from rainforest birds, and is decorated with a pattern of dragons chasing the sun.

# BELIEFS AND IDEAS

In Charlemagne's time almost everybody believed in the existence of gods, spirits or a single God. Life seemed very unpredictable. No one knew when they might be killed in battle or by a terrible disease. Religious faith was the only way people could explain the world around them. Scientific ways of explaining things, from why the sun shines to how germs can kill us, had not yet been discovered. Religion also set down rules for living that held a community together. Even though many rulers, including Charlemagne, often quarrelled with religious leaders in their lands, they still believed in the gods and their powers.

## CHRISTIANITY

EUROPE

Like many people in western Europe, Charlemagne was a Christian and belonged to the Roman Catholic Church. In eastern Europe, and in the Byzantine Empire, Christians belonged to the Orthodox Church. The two Churches had different leaders and worshipped in different ways, but they shared the same beliefs.

▶ The Moone High Cross was carved in Ireland in about 800. Crosses were used to mark churchyards and other Christian sites. In remote Celtic countries, like Ireland and Scotland, the Christian church had its own traditions of art. A circle with a cross is a typical Christian Celtic design.

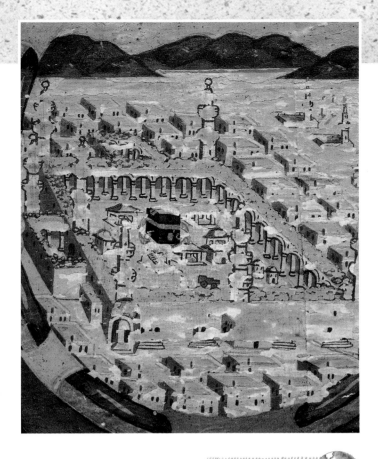

► The holy city of Mecca, painted in the 800s. The Prophet Muhammad received his messages from God while praying in the mountains close to Mecca.

## MONKS AND NUNS

In Europe there were many Christian communities, called monasteries and nunneries. Here men and women spent their lives praying to God, and studying the Bible. Many monks and nuns became famous for their wisdom and holiness. Alcuin, who worked for Charlemagne, was an excellent scholar and teacher. St Boniface (who lived from about 672 to 754) spent his life travelling around northern Europe trying to teach people about Christianity.

## GODS OF THUNDER AND WAR

Vikings and Saxons worshipped many gods, including Thor, the god of thunder, and Odin, the god of war and wisdom. Many Viking men wore lucky charms shaped like Thor's thunder-hammer round their necks. They also believed that if they died in battle their souls would go straight to Valhalla. This was the palace of the gods, where they would spend eternity eating, drinking and listening to stories of brave heroes.

◄ A Viking tombstone, decorated with pictures of a Viking ship (bottom) and the god Odin riding Sleipnir, his magic eight-legged horse (top right).

## A NEW RELIGION

**MIDDLE EAST**

Islam was a new world religion in Charlemagne's time. Muslims believed that the Prophet Muhammad, who lived from around 570 to 632, had received messages directly from God. These told people the right way to live and worship. Muslims were eager to spread news of God's message wherever they went. When Muslim armies set out to conquer new territories, preachers travelled with them. The faith of Islam quickly spread to many lands.

## RELIGION AND POLITICS

In Charlemagne's time religious and political arguments were often mixed together. The Muslim rulers of the Middle East and the Christian rulers of the Byzantine Empire were fierce political rivals. They fought to control the rich trading cities and important shipping routes in the Mediterranean. The fact that they followed different religions made their quarrels worse.

## SPIRITS AND FAMILY ALTARS

In North Africa there were communities of Christians, Muslims and Jews. In many other parts of Africa, people followed traditional beliefs. These varied from nation to nation, but they often shared important ideas, such as a belief in the power of the spirits who lived in all created things. These spirits could drive away sickness or bring peace. Many families also made offerings to their ancestors at household altars or at family graves. They believed their ancestors could help them to live a rich and happy life.

## ANCIENT INDIAN FAITHS

In India most people were Hindus, a religion that had grown up around 1500 BC. Hindus worshipped many different gods and goddesses, such as Vishnu the Preserver, Shiva the Destroyer, and Ganesh, the elephant-headed god of wealth.

Another important religion in India was Buddhism. It was started in India, in about 550 BC, by an Indian prince called Siddhartha Gautama, who became known as the Buddha. Buddha taught that each person should try hard in life to do good works. They should also spend time thinking about good, holy things. Buddhism attracted many new worshippers in south India and Sri Lanka in Charlemagne's time.

► The Great Buddha statue at the Todaiji Temple in the city of Nara, Japan. It was made between 745 and 752. Stories tell how the statue was cast from melted-down bronze mirrors given by noblewomen.

## BUDDHISM IN CHINA

For hundreds of years people in China had followed either the Taoist or the Confucian faith. Both were based on the teachings of Chinese religious leaders who had lived in about 500 BC. But after about 100 AD, monks from Central Asia began to teach Buddhist beliefs, and many Chinese people, from emperors to peasants, became Buddhists.

Between about 550 and 800, Chinese forms of Buddhism spread to Japan. There they combined with Shinto, the ancient Japanese religion, to form a new set of beliefs. Buddhism was popular in China until 845, when it was banned by the emperor because he thought that Buddhist scholars and religious leaders were becoming too powerful. After 845 Chinese people began to follow Taoism and Confucianism once again.

## RESPECT FOR NATURE

Different North American nations had their own traditions and religious rituals, but they shared many similar beliefs. Most people believed in powerful spirits who could be contacted, for good or evil, by magicians and healers called shamans. They also respected all living creatures and the natural environment.

▶ A Mogollon craftworker made this pottery bowl in about 900. It is decorated with paintings of a man and a woman. Bowls like this were buried as offerings to the gods. The hole in the bottom was made at the time the bowl was buried, to set its spirit free.

## OFFERINGS TO THE GODS

Like many American peoples, the Maya offered blood and human sacrifices to the gods. They hoped that in return the gods would keep people safe, send rain and make animals healthy and crops grow. Priests organized processions, with music and dancing, in the great open squares outside the temples. For the Maya, most everyday activities had a religious meaning. They said prayers and made offerings when they cleared fields, planted seeds or gathered the harvest. Sports and games had religious meanings too. In their most popular sport, the ballgame, a rubber ball was supposed to represent the sun rising and setting in the sky. Losing teams of players were sometimes killed as sacrifices to the gods.

## ANCESTOR SPIRITS

In Australia, Aboriginals believed that human beings were connected to all other living creatures and to the land itself. They had all been created in the Dreamtime by the Ancestors – invisible spirits whose power could be seen in certain places such as holy mountains and pools. Aboriginal peoples were organized into many groups, each descended from their own special Ancestor. Their beliefs were not written down, but handed on in traditional stories, paintings, dances and songs.

## NATURE SPIRITS

Many Pacific peoples worshipped nature gods and spirits who lived in dramatic, dangerous places such as waterfalls, volcanoes and the sea. They built altars to these gods, and gave them offerings of food. Pacific islanders also believed that the gods made certain people and places holy or 'tabu'. They had to be treated with special respect.

▶ This stone carving of a tabu (holy) figure may be either an ancestor or a goddess of the Pacific peoples. The figure has her hands raised as a sign of her power.

## PEOPLES FROM AROUND THE WORLD

# GLOSSARY

**Aboriginals** The first inhabitants of Australia, who arrived there more than 40,000 years ago.

**Anglo-Saxons** The people who lived in England. They were descended from invaders from Germany and the Netherlands who married the local peoples.

**Bantu** African people who spoke similar languages. They lived in West and Central Africa, but groups of them migrated south and east, to settle in new lands.

**Berbers** Nomads who lived in the dry lands of North Africa.

**Bulgars** People who lived around the shores of the Black Sea. They fought against the Byzantines.

**Byzantines** People who lived in the Byzantine Empire (see page 14). Byzantine rulers took over part of the old Roman Empire, in 474 AD.

**Celts** People who lived in Brittany, Ireland, Scotland and Wales.

**Franks** The people Charlemagne ruled. They lived in southern Germany and northern France.

**Inuit** Native Americans who arrived in the Arctic regions of North America in about 2000 BC.

**Magyars** Nomad people from Central Asia who migrated to settle in Hungary in about 900 AD.

**Maya** A civilization in the rainforest region of Central America, most powerful from about 250 to 900 AD.

**Maoris** Settlers in New Zealand who came from the Pacific Islands from about 850 to 900 AD.

**Native Americans** The first inhabitants of America, divided into many nations, with different languages and lifestyles.

By Charlemagne's time people had settled in the hot, dry south-west of North America, including the **Anasazi**, the **Hohokam** and the **Mogollon**. Others had settled along the fertile valley of the Mississippi River, while the **Algonquian** people hunted in the woods of the north-east.

In South America the **Chimu**, **Sican** and **Huari** had established civilizations in the Andes Mountains and along the east coast of present-day Peru.

**Pacific peoples** People who lived on islands in the Pacific Ocean. They were descended from settlers who migrated there from south and east Asia.

**Saxons** People who lived in northern Germany.

**Slavs** People who lived in eastern Europe. They fought against the Vikings, who wanted to capture them and sell them as slaves. The word 'slave' comes from Slav.

**Vikings** People who lived in present-day Scandinavia. They were warriors, traders, explorers, and skilled craftworkers. By 900, they had settled in Iceland, parts of Scotland, Ireland, eastern England and northern France.

**alliance** A friendly agreement between nations or peoples.
**architect** Someone who designs buildings.
**Aristotle** A Greek scientist who lived from 384 to 322 BC.
**astronomer** A scientist who studies the stars and the planets.

**barracks** Buildings where soldiers live.
**bearing-dial** A small sun dial, used to help sailors find the direction south at sea.
**Buddhism** A religious faith based on the teachings of the Buddha, an Indian prince who lived in the sixth century BC. He taught people to seek the right way to live through meditation.

**cacao** Fruit of a tropical tree.
**caliph** Ruler of the Muslim empire.
**camel-train** A group of camels carrying goods for a long journey(also called a caravan).
**chain mail** A type of armour made of metal rings.
**charcoal** Specially treated wood that burns at a high temperature.
**Christianity** A religious faith taught by Jesus Christ, a religious teacher who died in about 33 AD. Christians believe Jesus was the son of God.
**Church** The organization of the Christian religion.
**civilization** A society with its own laws, beliefs, and artistic traditions.
**convent** A place where nuns live.

**coral** A beautiful material formed from skeletons of tiny sea animals. An underwater cliff made of coral is called a **coral reef**.
**courtiers** People who spend time at a ruler's palace and give advice.

**dynasty** A series of rulers belonging to the same family.

**empire** A large area of land, including different nations, with a single ruler.

**fortress-town** A town surrounded by strong walls, often guarded by soldiers.

**glaze** A glassy coating used to waterproof and decorate objects.
**governor** A ruler of part of a kingdom or empire.

**harpoon** A spear used for hunting fish.
**Hindu** A person who follows the Hindu religion, which grew up in India between 1500 and 600 BC. Hindus worship many gods, but they are all forms of Brahman, the supreme god.
**homespun** Rough cloth, spun and woven at home.

**iron ore** Rock that contains iron.
**irrigation** Bringing water to dry lands along specially-built channels so that crops can grow there.
**Islam** The worship of Allah (God), taught by Muhammad, a prophet who lived in Arabia from 570 to 632 AD. Followers of Islam are called **Muslims**.
**ivory** The material elephant tusks and walrus teeth are made of.

**jade** A valuable greenish stone.

**lodestone** A naturally magnetic stone used to help sailors find the direction north at sea.

**manuscript** A book written by hand, often beautifully illustrated.
**medieval** The period of time from about 500 to 1500. Also describes things from that period.
**merchant** A person who buys and sells goods.
**migration** The movement of people in search of somewhere new to live.
**millet** A plant that produces grain.
**monsoon rainfall** Heavy rain that comes at the same time each year.
**mosaic** A picture made from little pieces of glass or stone carefully fitted together.
**mosques** Buildings where Muslims pray and study.
**mother of pearl** A hard, shiny substance found inside some shells.
**mud brick** Bricks made from mud and baked hard in the sun.
**Muslim** see Islam.

**navigate** To plot a course at sea and steer a ship along it.

**observatory** A building from which people study the stars.
**oil-palm** A tall palm tree. Its fruit is crushed to give oil.

**paddy fields** Flooded fields where rice is grown.
**pueblos** Native American villages made up of buildings like apartment blocks.
**philosophy** The study of ideas, knowledge and wisdom.

**pilgrim** A person who makes a special journey, called a pilgrimage, to visit a holy place.
**plantain** A banana-like fruit.
**possum** A small mammal found in Australia and the Americas.
**Ptolemy** A Greek astronomer who lived in the 2nd century AD.

**rebellion** Disobeying a ruler or government.
**reservoir** A large pool or tank built to store water.
**ritual** Traditional way of marking a special, often religious, event.

**scholar** Someone who spends their life studying and learning.
**scribe** A specially-trained person who kept written records or copied out books by hand.
**shipping route** A route across the sea followed by many ships.
**shrine** A holy place.
**slash and burn** A method of farming where people cut down and burn bushes, then plant crops on the cleared land. After a while they move on to a new area, leaving the bushes to grow back.
**smelt** To heat **iron ore** so that the iron is separated from the rock.
**sorghum** A grass-like plant with edible seeds.

**taxes** Payments of money or goods made to a ruler to pay for running the country.
**trading post** A place where people meet to buy and sell things.
**tribe** A group of people of the same race and culture.

**yam** A kind of root vegetable.

# INDEX